ANTLERS AWAY

CLOSE ENCOUNTERS IN THE DEER WOODS!

Bruce Cochran

WILLOW CREEK PRESS

Minocqua, Wisconsin

DEDICATION

For Carol
who puts up with it all

ISBN 1-57223-704-X

Published by Willow Creek Press
P.O. Box 147, Minocqua, Wisconsin 54548
www.willowcreekpress.com

Printed in Canada

INTRODUCTION

In the 1930s it was so rare to catch a glimpse of a whitetail deer in most parts of the country. The split hoof track, so familiar now to anyone who roams the woodlots (or even the suburbs) from Washington to Florida, was seldom seen.

Since that time however deer numbers have rebounded to astonishing levels. Recently an old timer in a small Midwestern town was asked if there were many deer in the area and replied, "Are there many deer around here?? Why son, they're coming into town at high noon, walking right down Main Street and peeing on the school bus tires!"

The burgeoning number of deer has brought with it many problems such as increased crop depredation and deer vehicle accidents. But it has also provided a tremendous increase in recreational opportunities. Now some 10.3 million* men, women and youngsters take to the autumn woods armed with everything from crossbows to center fire rifles in search of whitetails, muleys, and several lesser-known species. In some areas schools traditionally close for the opening of deer season. Otherwise respectable citizens call in sick in order to arrange an extra day off work to pursue that big buck or tasty doe.

This book takes a light-hearted look at those outdoorsmen and women and their families. The tree stand sitters, the stalkers, the rifle toters, the bow hunters, the gadget freaks, the old timers, and the novices who wouldn't know a 30.06 from a 747.

And let's not forget the deer. . . those elusive yet curious, intelligent yet often wacky residents of our fields, forests, farmlands, and in some cases our back yards.

*2001 national survey of fishing, hunting and wildlife associated recreation by the U.S. Fish & Wildlife Service.

PRE SEASON SCOUTING

CAN MAKE OR BREAK YOUR *Deer Season*

FIND A HANDY TAVERN

When your camp mates have heard all your hunting stories you'll want to drive into town and bore a new audience.

WHERE'S THE NEAREST
FAST FOOD RESTAURANT?

Wouldn't a nice cheeseburger taste better
than Uncle Bubba's road kill chili?

LOCATE THE
NEAREST HOSPITAL

When you fall out of your tree stand
you'll need immediate medical attention.

CHECK THE PREVAILING WINDS

You'll want to spend as little time as
possible downwind from your buddies
after a night of beer, beans and chili.

SELECT A LOCATION TO HANG YOUR STAND

Find an out of the way place,
far from any deer sign, and
you'll be guaranteed a good nap with
no untimely deer interruptions.

GET in SHAPE

FOR THE SEASON WITH THESE PRE-HUNT EXERCISES AND TUNE UPS!

Get in shape to drag that big buck out of the woods. Practice dragging your wife, (or some other heavy object), around your yard at least twice daily.

Hone the skill you'll rely on most. Stand in front of a mirror and practice lying with a straight face.

Get ready for those snoring bunkmates. Start a chain saw, place it on the floor close to your bed, then try to go to sleep.

Prepare your digestive system for deer camp food. Drop a semi-spoiled steak in the dirt, grill it till it's burnt on the outside and raw on the inside, then wash it down with a warm beer.

Practice makes perfect when tracking a wounded deer. Ask a friend to prick his finger, then walk through the woods leaving a trail for you to follow.

Practice answering the call of nature outdoors, from high in a tree if possible. No fair using toilet paper. Handkerchiefs and leaves only. Do not be self conscious if small animals watch you.

"It was owned by a little old lady who only drove it back and forth to her tree stand."

Deer Hunting
DEFINITIONS

Still Hunting

Often said to elderly deer
Hunters as in, "You old geezer.
Are you still hunting??"

SLUGS

What you take a few of
after the guns are put away.

RECOIL

What your wife does when you
tell her you're going to butcher
your deer on the kitchen table.

MID RANGE

The part of your body
that extends after eating
deer camp food for a week.

POPE & YOUNG

A Catholic youth organization.

DEER TAG

A personal license plate that
deer hunters put on their trucks.

CARTRIDGE

What your true love gave to you
on the 12th day of Christmas,
as in a cartridge in a pear tree.

FIELD DRESS

What ladies who hunted
used to wear into the field.

SHAFT

What you get when you
have to work on opening day.

QUIVER

What you do when the buck of a lifetime
appears twenty yards from your stand.

OVERDRAW

What happens to your bank
account when it comes time to
pay for the hunt of your dreams.

SCOPE MOUNT

A little stand to put your
bottle of mouth wash in.

BORE

A guy who tells the same
hunting stories over and over.

The rest rooms in the cafe are labeled BUCKS and DOES.

The town drunk sobers up for opening day.

There's a ten point buck hanging on the wall in the school principal's office.

They close the schools on opening day . . . so the TEACHERS can hunt.

The local hooker wears blaze orange hot pants.

The mayor is also the game warden.

You can buy doe-in-heat scent at the liquor store.

The cupids on the valentines shoot compound bows.

The high school football team's colors are blaze orange and camo.

You can buy a deer tag from the school crossing guard.

The first baby born each year is always named "Buck". (Even if it's a girl).

They force feed the raccoons water for two weeks before the season opens.

You can say, "Nice rack" to a woman without getting slapped.

You can bow hunt in the city park.

Bucks rub the velvet off their racks on the street light posts.

The local butcher processes more venison than beef or pork.

The high school girl's basketball team is called "The Fighting Does".

The local McDonald's has antlers instead of arches.

The fire chief uses the hook & ladder truck for a deer stand.

"Field Dressing Your Deer" is taught in kindergarten.

DEER CAMP NO NO's

No house slippers with
little bunnies on them.

No bikini briefs for hunters
weighing over 250 pounds.

When you sign your deer tag don't draw a little happy face on it.

Don't bring your wife's back issues of Good Housekeeping for the guys to read.

No Brandy Alexanders around the camp fire.

No canasta. No bridge.
No mahjong.

No playing cards
with flowers on the back.

No yogurt.
No tofu.
No bean sprouts.
No low fat ANYTHING!

No tassel loafers.

No quiche! Even if it's VENISON.

No Doilies.

WANT TO STOP DEER HUNTING BUT CAN'T DO IT ALONE? JOIN DEER HUNTERS ANONYMOUS!

When those crisp fall days roll around and you feel your will power cracking, call DHA! We'll send a fellow deer hunting addict over to drink with you until the season is safely over.

PEOPLE YOU'LL MEET IN THE DEER WOODS

BARRY BALLISTICS
Sure, it's good to know where your rifle is shooting but this guy is a fanatic! He's primarily interested in the size of his shot groups and enjoys sighting in more than hunting.

GARY GADGET
The equipment geek. Has all the goodies: GPS, laser rangefinder, high dollar optics, etc. Spends most of his time fiddling with his equipment.

FIDGETY FREDDY
He can't sit still. Goes back to camp for coffee at 8AM, says "Don't know why I didn't see any deer. I sat in my stand a whole hour."

SMELLY SMEDLEY
Douses himself with every scent product on the market. All at the same time! Smells like a horny raccoon with a urinary infection.

MR. COMPETITIVE
This guy has no time for fun.
He's SERIOUS! He pouts if he
doesn't hang the biggest buck
in camp every year.

PERCY PROTESTER
Roams through the woods banging on pots
and pans to scare deer away from the cruel
hunters. Wears leather sandals and buys meat
wrapped in plastic at the supermarket.

You Know You're a REAL DEER HUNTER When...

You go to a stag movie and you're disappointed when you see that it's about girls.

You can sleep as soundly in a tree stand as you can in your bed.

You think a see-through Teddy is a
scope mount named after Theodore Roosevelt.

You own a least one pair of
camo boxer shorts.

You know the term "broadhead" has nothing to do with Whitehouse interns.

You have no idea where the meat department of your local supermarket is.

You think Fred Bear's likeness should be carved into Mount Rushmore.

You have a ten point buck mounted on the wall........in your bathroom.

You send your Aunt Tillie,
(who's president of the local PETA chapter)
a package of venison liver every Christmas.

You wear blaze orange or camo
to the office on casual Fridays.

You leap to your feet when
Bambi's mom gets shot and scream
"The bitch had it coming!"

Your video library consists of
Monster Bucks of the Northland,
volumes 1 through 5.

All the new clothes you've
bought for the last ten years
have been blaze orange or camo.

Your kid says Santa's reindeer are up on
the roof and you grab your rifle or bow.

"I was cleaning it and it went off."

THIS HAPPENED TO ME!

CLOSE ENCOUNTERS IN THE DEER WOODS!

After drenching my clothes with doe-in-heat scent, I was attacked by a large buck. My fawn is due in February.

I used poison ivy for toilet paper and spent three days in the hospital. Remember that great Johnny Cash song, "Ring of Fire"? Well......

I drank too much and missed opening day, Thanksgiving, Chanukah, and Christmas.

While bow hunting suburban deer on a golf course I slipped on some goose poop, fell into a sand trap, and a bunny hugger whacked me with her nine iron.

After a big deer camp meal of beans and beer my scent lock suit exploded, setting fire to a forty acre corn field and peeling the paint off a nearby silo.

While asleep in my stand
a squirrel crawled into my
pocket, ate all my trail mix,
and threw up on my GPS.

I put on too much coon pee
and was kicked out of deer camp.

Designer SCOPE RETICLES

PEACE
For the old hippy hunter
who is still living in the 60s.

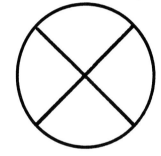

X-RATED
Let your mind wander to the
one thing you like even more
than deer hunting.

MERCEDES
For the upscale hunter who wouldn't
be caught dead looking at that big buck
through common cross hairs.

VORTEX

Stare into your scope and hypnotize yourself into thinking the buck of your dreams will appear any moment.

LIGHTENING BOLT

For the hunter whose shots never strike twice in the same place.

NO DEER

For the hunter who never sees a deer and doesn't need a reticle.

NEW GEAR, Gadgets AND GOODIES FOR THE DEER HUNTER

Your buddies will think you've bagged a deer even if you haven't when you display your PLASTIC GUT PILE.
Put it in the middle of deer camp and watch their expressions.

Didn't bag that monster buck?
Not to worry when you have an
**INFLATABLE
WALL MOUNT**

When nature calls while you're out in
the field you'll be prepared with your
**COMBINATION
FANNY PACK/PORTA POTTY**
Be sure to empty it before
you get back to camp.

Don't have your real teeth anymore?
You're better off without 'em!
A pearly white smile can be dangerous
in the deer woods. Be safe! Get
BLAZE ORANGE DENTURES
Also available in camo.

Take a stand as high as you want and
never lose consciousness with your
*TREE STAND
OXYGEN MASK*

Cover up your bad breath with something even worse. That big buck will be right in your face when he gets a whiff of your *DOE-IN-HEAT TOOTHPASTE.*

Now you can stalk those urban deer with confidence. They'll never know you're coming in your URBAN CAMO.

Tired of those yucky field dressing jobs? Now you can say goodbye to messy hands and bloody clothing. Just take a deep breath, point
ROBO-GUT
at your deer, hit the remote control, and stand back.

"BANG!! Just kidding."

AT LAST!

Bumper Stickers

FOR THE DEER HUNTER

BOW HUNTERS DO IT IN TREES

WHAT KIND OF RIFLE WOULD JESUS SHOOT?

COON PEE
It's not just for breakfast anymore

MY KID SHOT A DEER
WHILE YOUR HONOR STUDENT
WAS IN SCHOOL

NUKE PETA

Bambi
IT'S WHAT'S FOR DINNER

Designer Duds
FOR THE **DEER DUDE**

Getting married?
Your bride will be thrilled
when she sees you in your
*BLAZE ORANGE TUX
WITH CAMO TIE
AND CUMBERBAND.*

Want to be welcomed home from deer camp with open arms? Buy the little lady a *CAMO NEGLIGEE.* Available in Mossy Oak Breakup and Advantage Timber.

For the lady deer hunter
who enjoys some time at
the beach between seasons ...
*THE BLAZE ORANGE
BIKINI WITH OPTIONAL
SHELL LOOPS.*

Keep your neck warm and
dry in foul weather with your
GORE-TEX ASCOT.
Available in blaze orange and camo.

Get her in the mood for a romantic evening in the woods with your CAMO SMOKING JACKET.

Mo more problems with embarrassing flatulence when you have SCENT LOCK EVENING WEAR.

Enjoy a carefree stroll
through the woods in your
SNAKE PROOF
TASSEL LOAFERS.

When the fat lady sings
you'll know exactly how
far away she is with your
RANGE FINDER
OPERA GLASSES.

DEER HUNTING HAIKUS

Haikus are seventeen syllable Japanese poems consisting of three lines. There are five syllables in the first line, seven in the second, and five more in the third. You can make those lonely hours in a tree stand zip along much faster by composing your own haikus while waiting for Mr. Bigrack to appear. If your poem has sixteen or eighteen syllables it is not a haiku. It may not even be a poem.

Beans. Chili. More beans.
Tomorrow morning I will
hate my scent lock suit.

There he is! Huge rack!
In the cross hairs...oh, but wait!
Now I have to pee!

Deer can smell a man
miles away. I knew a girl
like that in high school.

Crunch! Crunch! Leaves rustling.
Deer? I turn slowly and look.
Hell no! Frigging squirrel.

Poker 'til midnight.
Alarm set for four AM.
Why do I do this?

Doe-in-heat scent. Coon
pee in refrigerator.
Muddy boots. Divorce.

Advantage timber,
Realtree. Mossy oak break up.
Now you can't see me.

Drag, stop, rest, pant, drag.
Now I wish I'd never shot
the son of a bitch.

Bob won't be with us
this morning. He got drunk and
fell into the fire.

I like rattling up
a buck. Blowing a grunt call
makes me have to fart.

Best food I ever
ate. You better say that or
you can cook next time.

Three days in this stand
and still no deer. If I was
a coyote I'd starve.

Full of chemicals.
Plastic wrapped. They call it meat.
No thanks. I'll shoot mine.

Four hundred yard shot.
Weighed three hundred pounds. Huge rack.
Twenty points. Bull shit.

Strong as acid, it
eats the paint off my pick-up
truck. Now THAT'S coffee!

Missed my only shot.
Bummer. No deer. Sad drive home . . .
CRASH! Now I've got one.

More new clothes? Not me.
I have blaze orange and camo.
What else could I want?

My toes are freezing.
I can see (and smell) my breath.
Is this fun or what?

So what's for dinner?
"Don't Ask, Don't Tell Chili". Uhhh . . .
Let's go eat in town.

High-tech underwear
wicking your perspiration
from you to my nose.

These eggs have too much
pepper. That ain't pepper. I
dropped them in the dirt.

Coon pee. Doe in heat.
Uncle Bob's sure fire buck lure.
I think I'll throw up.

Looking for deer sign.
Scanning the forest floor. Oops!
I just stepped in some.

Nice typical rack.
One of those big corn-fed ones.
Big buck? No, bar maid.

"... and now the Outdoors Channel presents,
Grunt Calls of the Rich and Famous!"

SPiKE BUCK, EDITOR OF GUT PILE MAGAZINE, ANSWERS YOUR QUESTIONS ABOUT DEER HUNTING!

Q: Do you ever have trouble dragging a deer out of the woods?
A: Only if he doesn't want to go.

Q: Should I rub coon pee on my clothes?
A: Whatever turns you and the little lady on.

Q: Do you have any Pope & Young or Boone & Crocket records?
A: No, but I have an old Caption & Tenille 8-track.

Q: What scope do you prefer?
A: Any except the one my proctologist uses.

Q: In heavy cover would you rather have a 180 gr. 30.30 or a 220 gr. 30.06?
A: I'd rather be under the covers with a 38-22-34.

Q: How many nights do you suppose you've spent in deer camp?
A: Not many. I usually sneak into town after the others guys are asleep.

Q: Do you ever use doe-in-heat scent?
A: Only as chili seasoning.

Q: Do you save your deer liver?
A: Are you kidding? I have enough trouble saving my own liver.

Q: Where's the best place to look for white tails?
A: Right above white legs.

Q: Do you prefer the heart shot or the neck shot?
A: I prefer the straight shot with a beer chaser.

Q: Have you ever tricked a buck into exposing himself by blowing a grunt call?
A: What do you think I am, some kind of pervert?

Q: Do you have any tips for field dressing a deer?
A: Of course. Make sure you have lots of string for your weed whacker.

Q: Would you carry a .300 Savage into the deer woods?
A: Of course. But, I'd rather she'd lose some weight first.

Q: Do you like to hunt during the rut?
A: Are you kidding? I'm too busy chasing broads.

Q: What do you think of the pivot mount?
A: Let's leave my sex life out of this. OK?

S. BUCK EDITOR

BALLISTICS MADE EASY

GOOD   BAD

"Your Realtree shirt clashes
with your Mossy Oak pants."

Deer camp ACCIDENTS

THEY CAN HAPPEN ANYWHERE, ANYTIME!

WEBSITES FOR THE DEER HUNTER

www.KoonpRus.com
Every smelly substance known to man is only a click of your mouse away.

www.gutpile.com
Answers FAQs about field dressing your deer.

www.rubnscrapes.com
Everything you need to know about deer sign and how to interpret it.

www.broadheads.com
The most complete bow hunting site on the internet. Not to be confused with **www.broads.com** a porn site.

www.deerdodads.com
Purchase useless deer hunting gadgets you never knew existed on-line.

www.fletchTHIS.com
Learn to make you own arrows on-line.

"Oh, no!"

THE RETURN OF Bambee

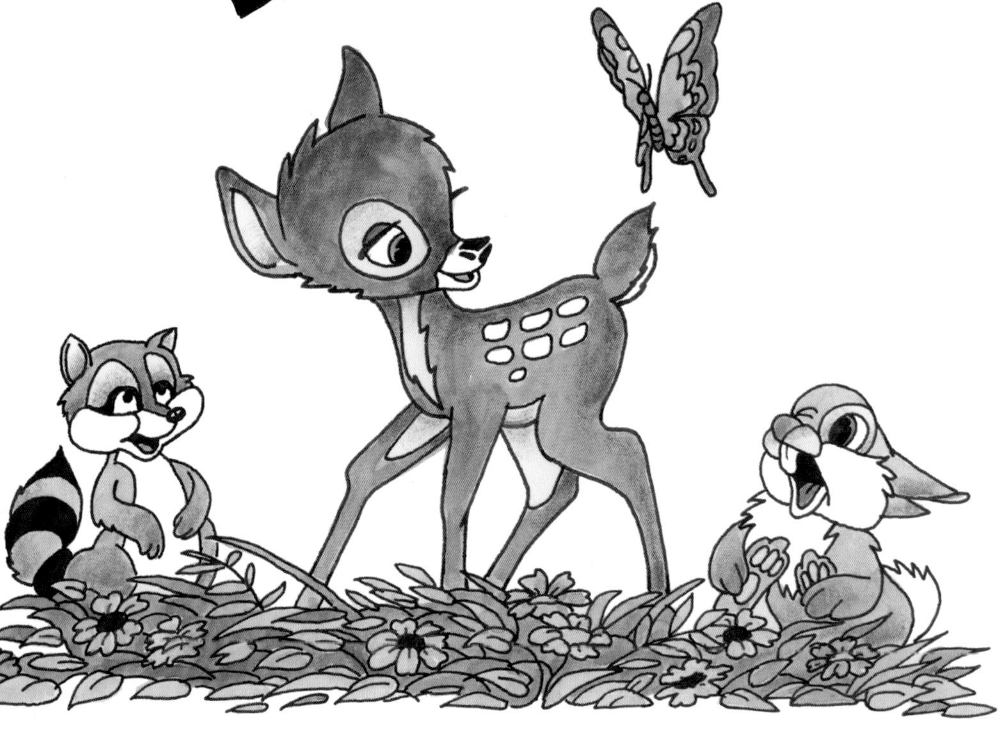

After a messy separation from his first partner, Faline, wherein Bambee is awarded court-mandated custody of the twin fawns on alternate weekends, he meets BIMBO, a sexy, flirtatious doe.

His neck swollen
with lust, Bambee throws
caution to the winds
and prances into a
clearing after his
new love,
where he meets . . .

...BUBBA,   and becomes...

. . . VENISON!

"Hey, I've got an idea! Instead of
all four of us playing solitaire . . ."

TYPICAL RACK

NON-TYPICAL RACK

NEW CALIBERS
FOR A NEW SEASON

ZERO CALIBER
VEGETARIAN SPECIAL
For the hunter who
doesn't like venison.

.38 MADONNA SPECIAL

.380 MOUSER

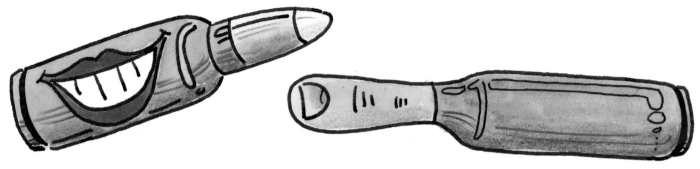

.257 JULIA ROBERTS

7MM PROCTO SPECIAL

30.06 SOFT POINT

.300 S&M MAGNUM

"Not tonight, deer."

25 THINGS YOU WILL

NEVER HEAR A DEER HUNTER SAY!

1. I don't think I'll shoot this 12 point buck. He's too big to drag back to camp.

2. Sure, this is fun. But I'd rather be back at work.

3. No big logs. This little camp fire is all we need.

4. Don't put any coon pee on my clothes. I smell bad enough already.

5. This knife is TOO sharp.

6. Put the camera away. We've got enough pictures of my monster buck.

7. You're right, Bob. Your buck IS bigger than mine.

8. It doesn't bother me that my son enjoys crocheting more than deer hunting.

9. No venison steak for me, thanks. I'm a vegetarian

10. I'm tired of hunting. I want to go home and repaint the kitchen.

11. Ya' know, I think the antis may have a point.

12. Everything I own doesn't HAVE to be blaze orange or camo.

13. You're right, Dear. I do spend too much money on deer hunting stuff.

14. Deer hunting is OK but it can't compare to bowling.

15. I know it's opening day but I've got a 7 AM tee time.

16. Who cares which way the wind is blowing.

17. Think I'll sleep in this morning. It's twenty degrees out there.

18. What's so great about opening day?

19. Let's wait 'til daylight to go to our stands. It's DARK out there.

20. Three rounds in a twelve inch circle. That's good enough.

21. Think I'll sell my bow and donate the money to PETA.

22. Why'd you bring that duct tape and those bungi cords? We'll never use THAT stuff.

23. You think this stand is TOO high?

24. Might as well toss these catalogs. I never order anything from them.

25. I can't stand deer camp food so, I brought along some TV dinners.

1. Count the points.

2. Measure tip-to-tip spread.

3. Divide numbers of points by buck's weight, using calculator if necessary.

4. Subtract circumference of
   main beam from above number.

5. Divide your weight by
   buck's field dressed weight.

6. Weight 'til the sun shines Nellie.

7. Throw rack in dumpster.
Next time shoot a doe.

The End